ECONOMICS

MAKING GOOD CHOICES

HOW TO STUDY ECONOMICS

DON MILLMAN

Itasca Community College

SOUTH-WESTERN College Publishing

An International Thomson Publishing Company

Acquiring Editor: Ken King
Publisher/Team Director: Valerie A. Ashton
Sponsoring Editor: Jack Calhoun
Production Editor: Karen L. Truman
Marketing Manager: Scott Person
Production House: Trejo Production
Cover Design: Birdland Design
Cover Photography: ©PhotoDisc
Internal Design: Craig LaGesse Ramsdell
Team Assistants: Ronda Faulkner, B. J. Parker, Cory Broadfoot

HB62AD
Copyright ©1996
by South-Western College Publishing
Cincinnati, Ohio

ISBN 0-538-85305-0

1 2 3 4 5 6 7 8 9 0 MA 4 3 2 1 0 9 8 7 6 5
Printed in the United States of America

IⓉP
International Thomson Publishing

Contents

Foreword to *How to Study Economics*

This Guidebook aims at helping you to learn economics efficiently and effectively. All higher education should help you to learn to think better, to think critically, with precision, clarity, and a depth that will help you to remember and understand concepts. Thus, what this Guidebook does is to apply economic thinking to topics of interest to students. You don't need to know anything about economics to understand this Guidebook, so you can read it before starting on the text—and then refer to it often during the term to improve study skills and test scores.

The first chapter of the Guidebook illustrates economic thinking by looking at your choice to attend college, then raises the question of what exactly is a *good* choice, and gives a quick overview of text features. Chapter 2 discusses how and why to use these special features in the text, and Chapter 3 argues that learning to study is a good choice. Also, Chapter 3 presents the well-known SQ3R method and shows how you can apply it to your economics textbook. Chapters 4 and 5 continue on the topic of studying, with special attention to graphs and to taking lecture notes. Chapter 6 addresses the not necessarily painful issue of taking tests (not necessarily painful if you apply the ideas in this Guidebook!) and how to improve test performance. Then the later chapters look at questions of particular interest to students—career choices, borrowing and saving, personal investing, and the idea that human capital is your most important asset. Throughout the Guidebook I have tried to show the relevance of economics, why and how economic thinking can be of use in everyday life, and why it is in your self-interest to study effectively, enough, and efficiently.

Chapter 1
Introduction:
Choices and Cuts

Economics is a powerful way of thinking. I wrote this booklet to help you learn and apply economic logic, to help you see the relevance of economics to your personal choices, and to help you improve your study skills.

Your Choice to Attend College

For an example of how economists think, consider your choice to attend college. You expect benefits from years of study, from money earned, and money borrowed to finance college, you expect benefits, including a degree and a good job for which a degree is a prerequisite. What are the costs of this choice to attend college? An economist looks at costs as the path not taken, the best possible alternative that you gave up to attend college. Perhaps you're giving up the alternative of earning $16,000 per year at a local factory, or the opportunity to join the Army, or the chance to go on the road with a rock and roll band. Here's the point: *You can't have it all.* To choose one alternative is to give up another and the cost of a choice is what we must give up.

What Is a Good Choice?

We live in a world of limits, including limits on time, information, and money, and limits set by natural laws and government laws. Bad choices often result from a failure to recognize limits, a failure often caused by wishful thinking or self-deception. Thus, it can be quite a challenge to make a good choice, a choice that takes into account the foreseeable costs and benefits of the action being considered. Because we live in a world of limits, we do not want to waste our precious time and money or other limited resources. In other words, we want to use the resources that we have efficiently, rather than to waste them. The economic way of thinking suggests that instead of wasting time and money by studying inefficiently, we should invest some resources (as you are doing now, by reading this booklet) to find out how to learn effectively. But is it worth your while to read this student guide? Is studying economics right now the best possible choice you could make?

The world is an uncertain place in which even information has costs; therefore we don't know enough to make the best possible choice in most situations. The most we can hope to do is to make good choices, to take actions that are likely to increase our happiness and well being. *Is* spending time reading this booklet a good choice for you? After all, there are plenty of other things you could be doing now, such as sleeping, studying something else, telephoning friends, or watching television. The first wisdom of economics is that *choices have costs*. To gain a benefit, you must give up some other good alternative. I don't know what you are giving up by deciding to read this guide to studying economics, so there is no way for me to know whether studying this material is a good choice for you. Only you can know the costs of a choice you make. On the other hand, the benefits of reading this booklet and applying the ideas you will find *can* help you learn from the textbook more efficiently, improve your test scores, and make economics more interesting and more relevant to making good choices in your daily life.

Quick Survey of Text Features

Let's take a quick look at some of the features of your textbook, *Economics: Making Good Choices,* to help you to learn to think like an economist and to study efficiently.

- On the first page of each chapter are the Chapter Learning Objectives, which tell you what you should be able to do after studying the chapter. Reading these objectives gives you a preview of what the chapter is all about and questions you should be able to answer after studying it.

- Important terms in boldface type, along with definitions and specific examples to illustrated the terms, are in the margins of the text pages. You can read this material in the margins as a running summary of the chapter, for review, and to reinforce learning as you read along in the text.

- Every few pages, the Concept Checks allow you to test your understanding of the main points. Try to answer each of these questions, then check your answer against the one given on the last page of the chapter. If you cannot answer correctly, reread the section of the chapter preceding the Concept Check.

- The Thinking Exercises can help to develop your critical thinking and writing abilities while increasing your understanding of basic ideas. *Doing* these thinking exercises can add much to make economics more interesting and to help you practice using economic logic.

- The Concepts in Action features in each chapter are specific examples from newspapers and magazines to illustrate economic ideas with stories about real people, events, and issues.

- Concept Map Summaries provide a quick review that shows how major ideas in the chapter connect to one another. Because ideas *do connect* to other ideas, understanding comes largely from constructing these links in your mind.

- The Discussion Questions can help to encourage thought and discussion. Many instructors want students to ask questions, but students often have trouble coming up with their own inquiries. These discussion questions give you a list of interesting topics you can raise in class, especially when the instructor says, "Are there any questions?"

Chapter 2
How and Why to Use Special
Features in the Text

Chapter Learning Objectives

The first thing to do in studying a chapter is to take a look at the Chapter Learning Objectives. Think of these objectives as essay questions, questions that you should be able to answer after studying the chapter. One of the best ways to take notes from a textbook with learning objectives is to write out answers to each of these objectives in your own words. Note especially the last learning objective on the list for each chapter; it says that you should be able to write a paragraph identification of each of the terms in boldface in the chapter.

What is an identification? And why is it worth your while to write these out in preparation for tests? The paragraph identification (so called because you can do it in one paragraph) is a basic tool of critical thinking and writing. Definitions matter, not the exact wording, but rather the meaning, the fundamental idea behind the definition, is what matters. If you try to memorize a definition word for word to store it in short-term memory without comprehension, you have fallen into a trap of inefficiency, futility, and frustration. Only after you think you understand a definition should you study it. But do you understand it?

One of the best tests of comprehension is the ability to go back and forth between general ideas (such as definitions) and particular, concrete, specific *examples* to illustrate the definitions. Always add a specific example when you make a generalization or define a term. If you cannot think of a specific example to illustrate a concept, or remember one from the text or classroom, then you probably don't understand the concept being defined. Practice in giving examples will help your writing, not only when you answer to test questions, but whenever you do academic writing. Giving an example helps to get the definition to stick in your long-term memory. You may forget the exact wording of a definition, but you are much less likely to forget the specific example. Then, if you can retrieve the example from memory, you have a good shot at reconstructing the definition, assuming that you've written it out and studied it repeatedly.

All right, now you have a decent definition and an example, and you have written a couple of sentences of your paragraph. What's next?

What comes next in an identification is a brief discussion to show the importance and relevance of the concept you have defined. If this word is an "important term," *what makes it important?* Why did I think it was worth including in the book? To show the importance of a term, explain how it connects to other ideas, and especially how it is connected to major topics. It is in making connections that we make sense out of and construct knowledge. Your efforts to relate one idea to others pay off in both improved memory and increased understanding. But where will you find definitions in the text?

Definitions

Definitions of terms are in three places. First, you can find a term, printed in **boldface**, and its definition (along with a specific example to illustrate the idea) in the margin of a text page. Then, in the main body of the page, the term appears again in **boldface**, along with its definition and a discussion of the concept. Finally, in the combined Glossary/Index at the end of the book, **boldface** terms are found, along with their definitions are in alphabetical order. Page numbers in **boldface** show where the concept was first defined and discussed. Other page numbers show later references, where the term appears again in relation to various other topics.

Concept Checks

What about the Concept Checks? What's the payoff to you if you read and try to answer them? Concept Checks provide a way of seeing whether you have understood basic ideas. They can stimulate thinking and active learning. If you get the same (or similar) answers as those given at the ends of the chapters, this check indicates that you have understood the material. If you cannot come up with any answers, or if your answers are quite different from those given, then there are a few possibilities. Perhaps you have had a great original insight about something neither I nor other economists have considered. I make no claim that the answers to these Concept Checks are the only possible right answers. Perhaps you misunderstood the Concept Check when you read it. Or, most likely, you did not understand some of the text material. If the answer given at the end of the chapter seems wrong to you, go back and study text material on the concept, then look again to see whether the answer I gave makes sense. If you still have trouble after restudying, then ask questions of your instructor in class or during office hours. Don't be shy about asking questions, because part of your instructor's job is to answer them, and if you don't ask any, then you may not be getting good value out of the class.

Thinking Exercises

Thinking exercises can encourage active learning. Merely reading or underlining is a passive activity. In contrast, by putting your own words on paper in answer to the thinking exercises you are constructing your own knowledge of basic ideas. In other words, doing these exercises develops your critical thinking skills while adding to your knowledge of basic economic ideas. Furthermore, writing in your book makes it your own, a joint project between you and me. Finally, you can use your answers (or sometimes your inability to find answers) as a basis for discussion and asking questions in class.

Concepts in Action

The purpose of the Concepts in Action features is to bring economics down to earth. The economic way of thinking can help us understand what is going on in the world, and these features illustrate how economic concepts can help us to understand people, events, and issues in the news. Studying the "Concepts in Action" boxes can help you to see the relevance and importance of the economic way of thinking. The idea behind these boxes is to boost both your interest in and your comprehension of economics by seeing examples of the applications of economic logic.

Concept Map Summaries

Concept Map Summaries provide a quick review of major ideas in a chapter. The arrows show how ideas connect to one another, and the circled concepts in **boldface** type are a reminder of the important terms in the chapter. These summaries are not a substitute for reading the chapter, but they do give a rapid visual organization of the material.

Discussion Questions

The discussion questions are near the ends of chapters, just before the answers to the Concept Checks. These are questions to think about on your own and to ask about in class. After studying the chapter, you will have the intellectual tools, the ideas, that can help to provide a basis for interesting and illuminating discussion of these topics. Economics is not a settled body of knowledge, a mass of information to memorize about formulas and graphs; economics is a *way of thinking* that can help us get better answers to important questions. To a large extent, learning economics means taking part in two kinds of dialogue. First there is the dialogue among various economists that has been going on for more than two hundred years and continues today. Second, there is the dialogue that goes on in your classroom, among students and between students and the instructor. The purpose of the discussion questions is to encourage learning economics through both of these kinds of dialogues.

Glossary/Index

The combined glossary and index at the end of the textbook makes it easy for you to find information. **Boldface** type shows definitions of important terms and the page numbers where the text first defines and discusses the terms. Take a few minutes to browse through the Glossary/Index. Note that the index includes not only glossary terms but also other topics and proper names. When should you refer to this material at the back of the book? First, you can quickly look up the meanings of terms you do not know or of which you are unsure. Second, you can find the various places where the text discusses a topic you need to know about.

Citations and References

Every now and then, you'll find a quotation or a statement in the text followed by some information in parentheses, for example (Reich, 1991a, p.37). You do not need to know the names and dates within parentheses. Rather, these are citations to the works of various authors. If you want to look up the original source for a quotation, look in the References section of the text, which is just before the Glossary/Index. Names of authors are in alphabetical order, and if there is more than one citation to a name they are in chronological order under the author's name.

Chapter 3
Why Learning to Study
Is a Good Choice

Studying as a Set of Good Habits

Have you ever watched a self-taught tennis player try to keep the ball in play? Or looked at someone typing with the hunt-and-peck method? Without some coaching, hardly anybody will develop a decent game of tennis, because what comes naturally (swatting with a lot of wrist action as if hitting with a fly swatter) is ineffective. Similarly, the person who types with two fingers, always looking at the keyboard, will type slowly and with many errors. To become a proficient tennis player or typist, you need to know the correct way to do things, and you also need to practice your skills to maintain a level of proficiency. Often, parents and teachers tell students to study *more*. Perhaps you do need to spend more hours at study. However, if your study habits and skills are weak, these extra hours will have large costs and small benefits. On the other hand, learning to study *more effectively* can have a large and long-term payoff in return for a moderate initial investment of time and effort.

What are some of the common mistakes that students make in studying? First, many students regard studying as a passive activity, whose goal is to soak up knowledge much as a sponge soaks up liquid. But people are not sponges, and words in your textbook are not spilled ink to be absorbed and stored as so many nonsense syllables in your short-term memory the night before a test. Symptoms of this passive approach to learning include excessive underlining or highlighting. Another ineffective technique is what I call the brute force approach to studying. One pass with the sponge didn't soak up much, so you read a chapter over and over, hoping that comprehension will come with repeated readings. Memorizing definitions word for word or trying to memorize a graph are other examples of common mistakes that reflect a passive approach to studying. There is a better way to study, and it has been around and proven for fifty years. What is this active approach to studying?

The SQ3R Method

SQ3R stands for *S*urvey, *Q*uestion, *R*ead, *R*ecite, *R*eview. This is the gold standard of study techniques, and it is probably the best one for you to use to master difficult material. You may already be familiar with this method from middle school or high school. SQ3R was developed by Francis P. Robinson in the 1940s, and it has stood the test of time and the challenges of many research projects to verify its effectiveness. Fads in education come and go, while SQ3R remains. Just as you are unlikely to develop on your own a better way of typing than professionals have discovered, you are also unlikely to find on your own anything as effective as SQ3R for studying. Here is a brief description of the method.

S *S*urvey: First, take a one-minute look at the chapter. Glance at the major headings and take a quick look at the Concept Map Summary near the end of the chapter.

Q *Q*uestion: Formulate *in your mind* one or two questions based on the first heading. (Do not write the question down at this point.)

R1 *R*ead: Read the first section to the end, and in your reading keep looking for the answer to the question (or questions) you have formulated.

R2 *R*ecite: Look away from the text and try to answer your first question in your own words. You can do this step either out loud (if you're not in the library) or by silently "talking" to yourself before you write a brief outline on paper. Your writing should be quite brief, just a few cue phrases including a specific example to illustrate each generalization or definition. There should be *absolutely no copying out of the book into your notes!* If you can't answer your question, then look back at the section a second time.

When you have a satisfactory answer to your question or questions from the first section, go on to the next headed section of the chapter. Then repeat the Question, Read, and Recite steps for each of the sections. After you get to the Concept Map Summary near the end of the chapter, spend a minute or two reading it, and then go on to the final step of SQ3R, described below.

R3 *R*eview: Look over your notes to get an overview of the chapter's main points and how they connect to one another. This step should take no more than five minutes. In addition to reviewing the questions you have asked, cover up your answers and see whether you can recite these answers to yourself without looking at your notes (or at the book). After self-recitation, check your answers against your notes.

Why does SQ3R work? It works because it is a method of *active* learning that turns studying from a boring, passive, ineffective attempt to be a sponge into a stimulating dialogue between the student and the author of the text. Just as learning to type or to play tennis takes practice, so does learning to apply SQ3R also take practice. The only hard part in step one, the *Su*rvey of the chapter, is to keep it down to sixty seconds. Turn the pages fast and discipline yourself to look *only* at headings. When you get to the Concept Map Summary, look at the **boldface** concepts in circles and the connecting arrows, but don't try to read words between the circled concepts. In doing this first step of rapidly surveying the chapter's material you will see the main ideas around which the chapter's discussion will focus. In other words, you are getting a look at the "forest" before you study the individual "trees."

For the second step, *Q*uestion, what you can usually do is to turn the heading around and make a question out of it if it is not already in question form. For example, the first heading of Chapter 1 in *Economics: Making Good Choices* is "Why Bother with Economics?" which is already in question form. The second heading is "Opportunity Cost," and this heading you can turn into several different questions, *all of them good ones.* The most obvious question is: "What is opportunity cost?" Perhaps a more interesting question is: "What does opportunity cost have to do with scarcity and choice?" Another question likely to stimulate thinking is: "Why do all economic choices have opportunity costs?"

If you have trouble trying to phrase a question, look back at the Chapter Learning Objectives on the first page of each chapter. You can easily turn these objectives into questions. For example, in the Chapter Learning Objectives for the first chapter, the second objective tells you that you should be able to *identify* concepts and then explains what is an identification is. Your question could be: "How can I identify the opportunity cost concept?" You can look at each term defined in **boldface** as a subheading, a topic about which you should ask yourself a question. Don't waste time trying to find the best of all possible wordings for a question. Note that questions usually begin with *What? How?* or *Why?* For some types of material, *Who? When? Where?* questions are appropriate, but when dealing with major concepts, it is usually best to stick with What? How? Why? to begin your questions.

Formulating questions is a skill, and there are two hazards to steer between while developing this skill. First, don't make your questions too broad: "What does opportunity cost have to do with choices, resources, land, labor, capital, entrepreneurs, managers, and secondary effects?" is just too big a question. On the other hand, don't make your question too narrow: "How is the concept 'opportunity cost' defined?" is too narrow and tempts you to focus on exact wording rather than on fundamental meaning.

In *Reading* the material you should actively search for an answer to your question. Thus, as you read, keep thinking back to your question and watch for the answer to it. Once in a while you will realize that the initial question you formulated in your mind for a section isn't adequate because it is too broad or too narrow.

What about *Reciting?* You should do this step immediately after reading a section, before you go on to the next section. Part of

12

How to Study Economics

reciting is using the Concept Checks and writing out answers to the Thinking Exercises. Self-recitation can also include writing out the answer to the question you have formulated, saying the answer to yourself silently, or saying it out loud. Merely reviewing the answer in your mind is not enough, because wishful thinking often causes us to think we have an answer when we don't. If you can recite an answer out loud, this will help it to stick in your memory, and for some people this step of hearing spoken words is essential for comprehension and remembering. When writing out your answer, be sure to keep it brief and to write from memory, *not* by copying out of the text. Don't write anything down until you have finished a section of a chapter, and then write only a few words. If you copy out of the book or write lengthy notes, you are wasting time and decreasing the efficiency of your studying. All your notes on a chapter should fit on half a page, or (if you write large and leave much white space) at most one page.

After you have read all the sections of a chapter, then it is time for the last step, a Review of the whole chapter. In this step you are checking to see whether you do understand the material and also reinforcing your learning. Look at the notes you have made on the chapter and compare it with the Concept Map Summary in the book. Then go through your reading notes section by section, where you have answers to the questions you have asked. *Don't stare at your answers or try to memorize them.* Instead, try to recite answers to your questions while looking away from your notes or covering up the answers you wrote. Can you give definitions and specific examples of the concepts used in your answers? If you can, then you've earned a ten minute break, so take one!

Modifications of SQ3R for Easier Topics

Some modifications to SQ3R can make it faster for easy material. Parts of *Economics: Making Good Choices* may be easy for you to understand, and here are a couple of ideas that can save you time. First, you can write your questions and answers in the margins of the textbook itself. This technique is very convenient and can save quite a bit of time. (Having information in only two places, textbook and separate lecture notes, is a lot handier than having information on a course spread out among text, lecture notes, and reading notes in a third location.)

A second possibility is to make *brief* underlinings and use code marks (star, single or double vertical lines) in the margin to make an outline of the answers you find in the text to your question. The method of using brief underlining and code marks to organize these underlined or highlighted passages requires frequent practice to develop a high level of proficiency. Effective marking of a book requires intense concentration and constant questioning of the importance and organization of the passage being marked. *Never underline a complete sentence. Never underline something that is already in italics or in boldface.* The text has already emphasized these items for you, and it's a waste of time to place additional emphasis on them with underlining. Use only a few code marks, such as a star by a major point, two vertical lines in the margin for a less important underlined point, and a single vertical line for a specific example. Then you can use SQ3R with underlining by modifying the last two steps as follows:

- *R*ecite your answer to the question you have come up with by saying the answer out loud or to yourself and then find the phrase or phrases in the text that answer the question. Underline these short cue phrases and mark them according to their importance in the margin. You should underline only *after* a section of the chapter has been read. Do *not* underline as you read.
- *R*eview by going over your underlinings and markings for the whole chapter.

If the underlining modification to SQ3R is to be effective for you, your underlinings and marks should be brief and clear enough so that you can review a whole chapter in about five minutes.

Your Personal Approach to Active Learning

Individuals differ in how they learn. For some people, reciting out loud is an essential step because these individuals rely heavily on the auditory sense for learning. If you are this kind of person, take advantage of your personal qualities and recite out loud. Others rely on writing to fix items in memory and to understand. If writing out material is essential to your understanding, then do not use the underlining modification to SQ3R.

For more information about how to develop study methods that work best for you, you might take a study skills class from the learning center at your college.

Chapter 4
Studying Graphs

Applying SQ3R to the Study of Graphs

Some students find graphs (and tables of numbers) so frightening or dull that they just skip them. You were not born with a hatred of graphs, and if you suffer from "graphophobia" (fear of graphs), it is an acquired fear. Perhaps the main reason that so many students find graphs about as pleasant to approach as rattlesnakes is that at some point in their educational history they were bitten by the "Know this graph!" command and then poisoned by trying to memorize meaningless lines, labels, and squiggles. SQ3R provides a way for people who are good at reading graphs to get better, and a way for the "graphophobes" to overcome their aversion.

To study a graph, you need two abilities. First you need to be able to *read* a graph, and then you need to be able to *answer a question* that you formulate about the graph. Here's how SQ3R helps to develop these two abilities:

- *Survey:* In this step, look at the titles of the graphs in a chapter. You can turn each of these graph titles into a question in the self-recitation step, as described below.
- *Read:* In reading graphs, pay attention to the title and the labeling of the lines on the graph. Formulate a question in your mind by turning the title of the graph into a question and then reading the graph to see how it answers this question. You should also read the text material near the graph and compare it with the graph.

Your eyes have to do some going back and forth between the discussion in words and the illustration of these ideas in the graph.

- *Recite:* In answering your question on the graph, you can either jot down some brief notes or underline the key phases in the text that answer the question.
- *Review:* After reading the whole chapter, go over all your notes, including the ones on graphs in the chapter.

A Critical-Thinking Approach to Graphs

Every graph is a model of reality, a simplification of ideas or data. In presenting graphs, what economists are trying to do is to make economics easier for students to understand. The graphs in your text have only a few lines. To understand what these lines mean, one of the most useful exercises you can do is to construct your own graphs one line and one label at a time. (For more on the study, construction and labeling of graphs, see the Appendix to Chapter 1 of your textbook, pages 14–16, titled "Words, Numbers, and Graphs.") By constructing graphs I do *not* mean copying them out of the book. Knowledge is constructed, not discovered. One of the best ways to construct knowledge of economics is to draw and label graphs for yourself.

When you label the axes of a graph, write out the labels in full, rather than abbreviating them, and ask yourself what they mean. Each axis represents a *variable*, something that can be more or less. As you draw and label axes, ask yourself what might cause changes in these variables. Another thing to ask yourself is: *What things are assumed to stay the same* in this graph? The variables of a graph, as shown by the axes, do change, but there are many other quantities that (by assumption) stay the same. Indeed, in many graphs *all* "other things" stay the same, as a curve on the graph shows how changes in the two variables on the axes illustrate a relationship between them. (Graphs that show a curve shifting from one position to another are exceptions to this rule.)

After drawing and labeling the axes of a graph, ask yourself how many lines are on the graph in the text. There may be only one more line, or two. At most, in the graphs used in your textbook, there will be three curves besides the axes. Here are two questions you should ask yourself about any line on a graph: First, *What does the label mean?* Second, *what does the line or curve look like?* The label of a line usually does not have a self-evident meaning. Hence, you should always consciously ask yourself as you write it down: *What does the label mean?* Then, again focusing on meaning and significance, ask yourself whether the curve on a graph slopes up or down as you read from left to right. Is the curve a straight line? Or does the slope of the curve change as you look from left to right, sometimes steeper and sometimes flatter?

Notice that on all graphs, a curve that slopes up shows a positive relationship. In other words, when one variable increases, so does the other one. If the graph slopes downhill (always reading from left to right), this downward slope shows a negative relationship between two variables. Thus the slope of a line on a graph is an important clue to its meaning.

Next, look at the points labeled on a graph, sometimes at the intersection of two lines. Ask yourself, *what is the significance of these points?* Why are these points labeled, and what do the labels on these points mean? If you cannot see the importance of labeled points on the graph, go back to your notes, your underlinings, or to the words on the page that explain the graph.

Finally, look away from the graph on the page and try to draw it one step at a time, labeled axes, labeled curves and points, and finally a title or caption. Trying quickly to reconstruct a graph a few times by drawing it yourself is far more effective than staring at a graph in a book and trying to memorize it.

Chapter 5
How and Why to Take
Lecture Notes

The Advantages of Taking and Using Lecture Notes

Taking lecture notes is a form of active learning that helps focus your attention and concentration in class. The act of note taking involves deciding what is important, deciding how to organize the information into major points and supporting detail, and doing the physical activity of writing words in your notebook. Students often complain that it is hard to pay attention in class, that the teacher is boring or rambles, or that lectures and classroom discussion are a waste of time. You get out of a class what you put into it. If you put more effort into taking notes, you'll likely feel that classes are of more value than if you just sit as a passive spectator.

Taking good lecture notes can add a lot to your understanding and (believe it or not!) to your enjoyment of a class. Using your notes to review frequently and comparing them to your reading notes will help you to learn the material without a lot of anxiety, stress, worry, and last-minute cramming. For that matter, just *having* good lecture notes will add a lot to your peace of mind. But as we shall see later in this chapter, you should review your notes often and not leave them to grow cold until the night before a test.

Why take lecture notes? Because if you do, you'll probably be happier, learn more, and get higher grades.

A Simplified Outline Approach to Note-Taking in Class

There are many systems for taking notes, including a few very good ones. The technique described below is my version of what many books on studying call the simplified outline method. (To learn about other ways to take classroom notes, look through some of the books in your learning center about how to study, or take a "How to Study" class.)

First, a few preliminary remarks. Make great efforts to attend every class and get to class on time. If you can get to class a couple of minutes early, glance at your notes from the previous lecture. Even a sixty-second review can do a lot to refresh your memory and get your mind in gear for the ideas your instructor is about to present. Take notes on white paper in black or dark blue ink. The easier your notes are to read, the better. In the classroom sit where it will be easy to see and hear the instructor. Watch your teacher closely as well as listening attentively. Most instructors, intentionally or unintentionally, use a number of gestures and other kinds of body language to emphasize important points.

All right, you're seated in your favorite seat, close to an exit (where an open door lets in plenty of noise), next to a window with a beautiful view to help you relax by gazing at it all during class, and among friends, so you'll have someone to talk to during class, and you're in the back row, where you can safely read the textbook for the class in which you have a test next hour, so you're all set. *Just kidding!* What is the first thing you write in your notebook? The date. Write the date at the very top of a new sheet of paper and then the page number "1" to indicate the first page of one day's notes. I put dates and page numbers on the far right-hand side of the page, as you would for a letter. Now what?

Often an instructor will make a few brief remarks to review the material of the previous class. Pay close attention to these words, but do not write them down in your notes. What you should be listening for is the main topic (or the first main topic) that the instructor will cover in *this* day's class. When you think you hear the topic that will be covered, write it out on the first line of your notebook paper, starting at the left margin. The topic name can be as brief as one word, or as long as a couple of short sentences.

You should write the first subheading indented under the main topic. Skip a line after the main topic and indent at least two inches from your left margin for this subheading, which can be either a phrase (sentence fragment) or a key sentence, or possibly a graph. If there is a specific example or some factual detail to support this first subheading, skip another line. Then indent at least another inch, so that the supporting detail is all on the right-hand side of the page. *Use lots of white space.* Your page should have more white space on it than writing. General points go on the left, and more specific detail goes on the right. Refer to page 22 to see what a page of lecture notes might look like for a lecture on opportunity cost:

In this system of note-taking you don't have to worry about Roman numerals or upper case and lower case letters of the alphabet. Also, *you don't have to spend time wondering whether something is a subtopic of something else and how to label it.* General statements go on the left, and more specific statements go on the right. There are only three levels of generality:

1. the big, broad main topics that you write across the whole page,
2. somewhat less general topics that are indented a couple of inches,
3. specific detail that is written on the right hand side of the page.

Instead of numbering, you can use white space and arrangement of material on the page to organize information. Capitalization and correct punctuation help to identify complete sentences, and you can use them as time permits, but often you will have time to write only in phrases. Putting main headings in sentence form is useful for later comprehension, but examples and supporting detail can usually be in phrases or lists with no loss of meaning.

Note the sparing use of abbreviations in the example of lecture notes on the preceding page. I abbreviated the date and used "e.g." in place of "for example," but I didn't use any other abbreviations. The problem with abbreviations is that you can forget what they mean. Even worse is the tendency to write down abbreviations without thinking of the *meanings* of the concepts being abbreviated. (Some books on studying recommend extensive use of abbrevia-

Opportunity cost -- what is given up when a choice is
    made because of scarcity, all choices have
    opportunity costs
        example -- giving up sleep to attend class

    opportunity costs are subjective
        for some people opportunity cost of attending
        class was giving up sleep, for others it was
        giving up breakfast or studying or work

    opportunity cost is highest valued
        alternative given up among things forgone
        alternative cost is another name for
        opportunity cost

"cost" in accounting not the same as opportunity
cost
        e.g. cost of using land owned by a firm not
        counted in accounting costs but is an opportunity
        cost because of giving up income from rent

opportunity cost is based on expectations of future
outcomes, not based on historical costs

only choices have costs because things do not have a
cost (something given up) apart from actions.

tions. I think this is bad advice. The main task of note-taking is the critical thinking function of deciding what is important, and you should not mechanically try to take down every word in some kind of shorthand, as stenographers do.)

When the lecturer finishes, make some large and distinctive mark at the end of your notes to show that this is the end of one day's lecture. If you get in the habit of doing this, it will save you the trouble of writing the date at the top of each fresh sheet of paper. On the other hand, if you use loose-leaf paper and three-ring binders for your notes, put the date at the top of each sheet of paper. Each day's notes start with a new page 1 and end with your distinctive mark.

If you get tired of lugging pounds of notebooks around with you from class to class, you can keep a week's worth of notes in one slim three-ring binder for all your classes. Then you can transfer these notes to a fat binder at home.

Now, what should you be writing down in your notes? First, most obvious and most important, are announcements having to do with assignments, dates of tests, and what material an examination will cover. This information may be in a handout that you got on the first day of class, but instructors often modify schedules as the term goes along. (I wish I had a nickel for every time a student has told me, after blowing a quiz: "I studied the wrong chapter.")

You should include main points and present them in your notes to make it clear that they are the main points. If you have trouble identifying which points are the major topics, watch and listen to your instructor as closely as possible. A good instructor will give you many cues, and even a less organized or less experienced teacher will usually indicate in some manner a transition to a new major topic. Often, the instructor will repeat main points. Definitions are often major topics.

You should take down anything written on the chalkboard or presented with an overhead projector. Do not, however, fall into the lazy person's bad habit of including in your notes only such material. Listen carefully for the instructor's comments on this material, and put that into your notes as well.

Include lists of items, specific examples, and supporting detail and explanation. Recall that the more specific material should go on the right-hand side of the page. The most general points related to this supporting material go across the whole page, and subheadings are indented two inches.

You should draw graphs in your notes. Be careful to label the graphs accurately and completely, and *make sure you know the words that correspond to any abbreviations used in labeling graphs.* One of the main reasons students have trouble with graphs is that they do not know the meanings of the abbreviations that label them. Does "PP" on a graph stand for "potential profit," "perfect price," or "production possibilities"? Your notes should include the meanings of abbreviations used by the instructor.

When, How, and How Often to Review Lecture Notes

Ideally, a student would review lecture notes every day, and serious students sometimes do this. Reviewing notes about twice a week is a more realistic guideline for most of us. You will need to study difficult material more often, and easy material you can put aside for a week between reviews. During the three or four days before a major test, you should review lecture notes each day. The main point is to review your notes regularly and often.

Should you try to memorize your notes? Positively not! With frequent reviews you'll be able to remember almost all the material you have taken down, but it is a waste of time to try to memorize notes word for word. Furthermore, attempts at rote memorization often lead to memory blocks and panic at exam time. What happens if you try to commit material to memory word for word, and then you forget one key word? What can happen in these cases is that you become fixated on the forgotten material and block out other knowledge. As a result, you can lose access to most of what you memorized when the recall of a few words fails.

When you go over your notes, you should be thinking about what they mean, whether they shed light on the real world, how they connect to ideas raised earlier in the course, and how they compare to the material you have studied in the text. Thus, studying notes becomes an active way to learn rather than being a grim and dull task. Going over notes shortly before bedtime helps many students to remember and understand. If you review notes often, then each review can be a quick one. You can read a week's lecture notes for one class in only a few minutes, *if* your notes are legible, *if* they make sense to you, and *if* you organized them well.

What about gaps in your notes? What about things you wrote down that made sense at the time but that you do not understand when reading over them? What about things that seem to be just plain wrong in your notes? In all of these cases, mark the questionable part of your notes, and try to find the topic in your textbook to clarify what seems to be missing or obscure. Often the text can clear up what is muddy in your notes, especially definitions. When reference to the text does not help, ask the instructor, either in class or during office hours, to explain the point that is puzzling you.

Chapter 6
Taking Tests

When and How Much to Prepare for Tests

Taking lecture notes, reviewing them, and using SQ3R for studying the text are the basic ways you can prepare for tests. There are two big points in regard to studying: First, you should study often; this is the idea of spaced (or distributed) learning. Second, you should study *enough*. Let's first take a look at the idea of spaced learning.

When you study for a class often, say two or three times a week, then the material can always be fresh in your mind. Also, when you study frequently, you need to spend only a short period of time at each study session. We live by the clock, and it is convenient to divide study time into one-hour blocks: fifty minutes of studying and ten minutes of break time. When you study often, then you can avoid the bad habit of cramming, which is trying to learn large masses of new material the night before a test.

Cramming is an inefficient and ineffective way to study for several reasons. First, most people find it difficult or impossible to learn large amounts of information in a single session. Furthermore, the procrastination involved in the habit of cramming adds to stress, worry, and fear of tests. Finally, staying up all night to cram means you'll be so sleepy on test day that you may be too groggy to do well. Many students say they have to cram, because if they study days or weeks in advance of a test they will just forget the material. *Bunk!* Overwhelming and compelling evidence exists to prove that spaced learning is far more effective for doing well on tests than is cramming.

So how often should you study? Several times a day is ideal. Even reviewing lecture notes for just a minute before class helps a lot. In a fifteen-minute block of time you can review notes for several lectures or for two or three text chapters. You can efficiently study new material with SQ3R in fifty-minute blocks of time. My advice is never study for more than three hours (including two breaks of ten minutes each after each fifty-minute block of time) at a stretch. I think you also deserve a ten-minute break every time you finish studying a chapter with SQ3R. This short break will help the material to gel in your mind and hence increase understanding, reduce forgetting, and make the transition to new material much easier.

Now for the question, *how much should* you study? This is a question to which I can give only general guidelines. Many colleges recommend that you should study for two hours outside of class for each hour of lecture. On the average, for a typical student in a typical class, this guideline is appropriate. But you are not a typical student (I've never met one), and the class that you are taking may be harder or easier than the average class. If it turns out that six hours per week of studying is enough to get the grade you are aiming for in a three-credit class, then stick with this guideline. If you have to spend much more than six hours per week to get a grade of "C" in a three-credit class, then something is wrong. Either you are studying inefficiently, or you are not ready to take the class. If a class is beyond your ability, then bail out rather than crash and burn. If your study habits and techniques are ineffective, then study and apply the preceding material in this booklet or take a study skills class.

Suppose you find that you can get high grades and feel confident about understanding the material while studying less than two hours for each hour of lecture, what then? Then you've got an easy class, and you can use the time saved by studying less for this class to study more for the tougher ones.

How to Prepare For and Take Multiple-Choice Tests

One of the clearest findings of research on studying is that students do better on multiple-choice tests when they study as if they expect essay tests. Why is this? What happens if students look at definitions, graphs, and facts as isolated little chunks of knowledge to cram into short-term memory to answer objective questions? What happens is that studying tends to become an ineffective effort at rote memorization. In contrast, by studying to be able to write answers to essay questions, students engage in higher order thinking skills. Thus, when studying for essay tests, students learn specific information needed to answer questions that show connections between definitions, graphs, public issues, and specific examples that illustrate generalizations. Hence, studying to answer essay questions results in an active effort by students to *organize* knowledge. This activity is much more effective for learning than attempting to memorize bits of information as an unorganized heap of facts and definitions.

With enough studying and effective study techniques you can become ready to take tests, but what happens when the test papers are being handed out and your palms are beginning to sweat? How can you use what you know most efficiently to get good test scores on objective tests?

Always read the instructions to the test at least twice, and underline important parts of test instructions. If you do not understand the instructions for taking the test, be sure to ask for clarifications. Tests have time limits, so you should make good use of this scarce resource of time. Figure out how much time you have for each part of the test, and then budget accordingly. For example, if you have fifty questions to answer in fifty minutes, then (on the average) you will need to answer one question per minute. Keep watching the clock or your watch, and every ten minutes or every fifteen minutes check to see that you are keeping up with the pace needed to finish the test in the time available. *Never* spend more time than you have budgeted on a question the first time you go through a test. After you have quickly answered the questions to which you do know the answer, then you can go back to ones about which you are uncertain.

In answering multiple-choice questions, try to visualize the answer in your mind as soon as you have read the stem of the question and before looking at any of the alternatives. Then read over each of the alternatives to see which one most closely matches this mental answer of yours. Do *not* spend a lot of time puzzling over what is the "right" answer in the sense of looking for some deep, final, complete truth in one of the alternatives. Rather, ask yourself: "What are they (your instructor and the author of the textbook) fishing for?" Each question tests for some evidence that you have studied and understood the assigned material. Rather than wasting time over deep philosophical issues of truth, keep asking yourself what your instructor is looking for.

For some multiple-choice tests, there are some tricks you can use to guess many of the correct answers, even if you don't know them. For the test bank of multiple-choice questions that I wrote to accompany the textbook, I was careful to make sure that none of these tricks would work. Each alternative, "a," "b," "c," and "d" is equally likely to be correct, regardless of the answers to preceding and following questions. The longest answer is correct one fourth of the time, not all the time. Some answers that contain the word "always" or "never" are correct answers. There are few, if any, questions to which you can guess the correct answer merely by eliminating obviously wrong responses. In other words, if your instructor uses the questions I have written, you'll just be wasting your time by trying all the old tricks.

In taking multiple-choice tests, be sure to put down an answer for each question. If there is a question that you are not sure of, mark it and come back to it later. Use any time left over at the end of the test to review answers of which you are unsure. Contrary to popular belief, most students who change answers are much more likely to change from incorrect to correct answers than to do the opposite.

How to Prepare For and Take Essay Tests

As suggested above, the best way to prepare for multiple-choice tests is also the best way to prepare for essay tests. There is no particular mystery about how to prepare for essay tests. First, take good lecture notes, use SQ3R for your textbook, and study your notes often. On essay tests, the best surprise is no surprise, so as you study, you should be constantly anticipating possible questions. Does your college library keep a file of past exams? If so, be sure to use this file. The same questions keep coming up again year after year, sometimes with similar wording, sometimes in different words. Hence, if you can see the questions that your instructor gave in the past, then you have a pretty good idea of what to expect. The Chapter Learning Objectives in the text give a sample of possible essay questions. Indeed, if you can give good answers to all these objectives, then you can write solid answers to *any* fair essay questions based on the textbook.

Preparation for essay tests in terms of using SQ3R, taking good lecture notes, and reviewing notes often is the same as preparation for taking a multiple-choice test. One thing that may be more difficult in taking essay tests than objective tests is budgeting your time. Here's a technique for efficient allocation of time on tests. First, figure out how much time you will have to work on a test. Handing out the papers takes some time, and you should also allow three or four minutes for reading the test before beginning work on it. Check to see how many points are on the test. Suppose (to pick an easy example) that you have a fifty-point test and fifty minutes to answer the test. Budget your time at one point per minute. Thus a ten-point question will get ten minutes, a five-point question only five minutes, etc. Next, mark on your paper the times at which you should begin work on each question. For instance, suppose you start work at 11:07 A.M., and the first question you answer is worth ten points. After you spend ten minutes on that question, it will be 11:17, and so you should begin answering the second question at that time. Make a note by each question of what time you should begin your answer to the question. If you are working a little ahead of schedule, that's fine, because you should try to budget a few minutes for proofreading after you finish writing the whole exam. Suppose, however, that you come to 11:17 and you're only half finished with your answer to the first question. What should you do then? Leave some blank space, *then go on to the next question.* No matter how much you write on the first question, you can get only ten points, and if you do not get to a later question, you will get a zero on that one.

If the test is, say, 120 points, and you have fifty minutes to complete it, then you need a bit of simple arithmetic to allocate your time efficiently. (You should not need a calculator to do this!) Divide the number of minutes by the number of possible points: 50 divided by 120 is equal to a little more than 0.4. Budget your time at four tenths of a minute per point. If you have a twenty-point question, just multiply the twenty points by 0.4 to get 8 minutes, and then you will know you can allot only eight minutes to that question. At first this technique may seem too complicated or require too much time. With practice, however, you can budget your minutes and write down the times at which you should begin questions in ninety seconds to two minutes. *This brief period can be the most important time you spend in taking an essay test.*

Budgeting time is especially important for good students. Those who don't know much often walk out of a test in less than half the time allowed. Good students generally know far more than they can possibly write in the time allowed, and it is human nature to want to show all that you know on a topic. The surest way to blow an essay test (aside from not studying) is to write all that you know on a question, regardless of time limitations. Hence, I cannot overstate the importance of budgeting time on essay tests.

Time is a scarce resource, so how can you use it most efficiently? First of all, *think before you write.* One of the commonest mistakes students make is to plunge into writing immediately, sometimes before they have even read the instructions for taking the test. If you have your thoughts well organized, then you can write far more effectively and efficiently than if you simply start writing at top speed whatever might be relevant to the question. Thinking before you write includes reading the question two or three times. As you read and reread the question, ask yourself what the question is about, what the examiner is looking for, what definitions and examples you might use in your answer. As with multiple-choice questions, keep asking yourself what the instructor is looking for in asking the essay question. Your concern is not what the "right" answer is in some absolute and final sense, but rather with what answer the instructor is hoping to get to a particular question.

Restate the question in your own words. Restatement of the question is a definition of the problem that you are about to answer. Your restatement of the question can be the introductory sentence of the first paragraph you will write in your answer. Why is this step worth doing? Because in redefining the problem in your own words, you are clarifying and focusing your thinking, and you're also coming up with a first sentence for your first paragraph. Well, what about a second sentence for your first paragraph?

In the second sentence, *state your main point* (also called a thesis statement). This main point is what you are going to defend and justify and explain in the rest of your answer. Now, does all this sound like something you learned in an English class? I hope so. One of the surest paths to success in writing essay answers is to do what your English teachers have been telling you to do for many years. Economics is not English, but to write good answers to essay questions in economics you need to use the conventions of correct writing.

Think and write in paragraphs. At first, this advice may be hard for you to follow. How can you "think in paragraphs" when you're nervous, under time pressure, and have a lot of information swirling around in your mind? The short answer is practice. Writing is a skill, like any other, and you will get much better with practice. *Always write in complete sentences.* This point is so obvious that I should not have to state it, but many of my students turn in masses of words in sentence fragments or in giant chunks of run-on sentences.

Use correct capitalization and punctuation. Again, do not let time pressure get in the way of writing sentences in proper form. So far as you are able, *spell words correctly and use proper grammar.*

Now, why is it worthwhile to write in correct English, using complete sentences, and organizing information into paragraphs? It's worthwhile because of time limits, and because the most efficient use of your time in writing essay answers includes using good English. Writing poorly wastes time because it does not get your answer across effectively. Bad writing reflects sloppy thinking, while good writing makes a positive impression on the reader.

"Oh yeah," you might say, "there just isn't enough time on essay tests to worry about writing in sentences and paragraphs. Anyway, instructors grade by the word, and the more words I put down, the higher the grade I'll get." Don't you believe it! Some of the worst essay answers I have ever read were the longest ones. Many excellent answers are relatively brief. Rather than being concerned about writing the most words possible, you should ask yourself the following questions about your answers.

First, have you defined the economic terms that you are using? You will almost always get points for definitions. Second, have you used specific examples to illustrate each definition and each generalization that you use? Finally, have you drawn and correctly labeled graphs where graphs are appropriate?

Learning from Your Mistakes

Every quiz, every test, every final examination is a learning experience. Regardless of how you have done on a test, you should always go over it. Look at each question you missed on a multiple-choice test and each answer you wrote on an essay test. If you got a high score on an essay question, ask yourself, "What did I do right?" If you missed a lot of points on an essay question, then ask yourself how you could have improved your answer.

If you do not get test papers back, then you should schedule an appointment with the instructor to go over the test. There is always a reason that you did not get some points on a test, and if you can figure out what the reasons are, then you can do better on future tests. For example, if you missed questions because the material was not in your reading or lecture notes, then you need to take better notes. If your notes had the relevant material but you still missed a question, then you need to study your notes more often. If you misunderstood the instructions to a test, then you need to read and follow instructions more carefully in the future.

In going over your graded test, you can find out whether questions came from the text, the lectures, or supplementary assigned reading. Also, in reviewing your test you can see how well you were able to predict test questions. Were some of the questions a surprise to you? If so, why?

In reviewing your graded test, you may find a question that you think you answered correctly but that was marked wrong. Should you go charging into the instructor's office, frothing at the mouth, and demand justice? First, check the textbook to see whether your answer agrees with the information in the text. Also, check your lecture notes. Then, if you still think your answer was correct, it is quite appropriate to ask politely why your answer was marked wrong.

It is especially important to review the first test in a class. If your grade on this test is not up to what you are aiming for, then *immediately* make an appointment to see your instructor. Go over the exam in detail, question by question, and discuss with the instructor what you need to do to improve your performance. Tell your instructor how much you studied and how you studied, and ask for suggestions as to what you might do differently so as to improve performance. Many instructors will offer to help you (for example, by looking at your notes and making suggestions for changes) to prepare for the next exam. It may be that you have a problem with test anxiety, a learning disability, or deficiencies in reading skills, or in writing skills. For these problems, go to your college learning center and get help.

Chapter 7
Economic Concepts and
Career Choices

Uncertainty and Information

We live in an information economy. In earlier times most people were employed on farms or in factories, but today most good jobs require abilities to find and use information. Jobs that depend little on information skills tend to be low pay, temporary, part-time, and lacking in fringe benefits. If you were satisfied with this kind of job, then you probably wouldn't be enrolled in college. Information is necessary to make good choices in everyday life, in doing your job, and in finding one. Studying economics can help you to become proficient at handling quantitative information (numbers, graphs, formulas), understanding abstract ideas, and applying logic to real-world problems.

Uncertainty has always been a fact of life. But during the past three or four generations the pace of change has increased dramatically. This faster pace of change has increased the uncertainty we face. Your great grandparents lived in a simpler and (except for the probability of premature death) more predictable world. What does this increase in uncertainty mean? And can you make good choices if you cannot predict the future at all?

The short answer is that *no*, you cannot make good choices if future events are entirely random and utterly unpredictable. Despite the rapid pace of change in the world and the foggy patches of uncertainty we face, however, economic thinking can help us to make good career choices, as well as good choices in consuming, saving, borrowing, and getting an education. How is it possible to understand and cope with an uncertain future?

The big problem here is to make sense out of the world. The perspective of economics can contribute a great deal in helping you to understand the world, to separate long-term trends from brief fluctuations, and to evaluate the statements of people who claim to have the answers to life's uncertainties. Where economics can help is in finding general rules or principles that persist despite drastic changes in technology and society. None of the basic principles of economics is particularly hard to learn, nor do they require mathematics beyond simple arithmetic, and you can learn all of them in a one-term introductory course. We live in a complex world, but not a chaotic one, and to deal with this complexity of information, uncertainty, and change, there is no better preparation than a college course in introductory economics.

Critical Thinking Skills and Habits Applied to Career Choice

The reason that economics can do so much to help us make sense out of the world is that economics is critical thinking applied to an especially large and important sector of the world. Indeed, it is *only* through a study of economics that you can make sense out of this big and important part of the world.

What is the first question you should ask yourself in regard to career choice? The first question to be answered is not an economic question at all, but a philosophical and psychological question: *Who am I?* In other words: What do I enjoy doing? What am I good at? What are my strengths and weaknesses? What is important to me? What kinds of activities give me a sense of meaning, purpose, and fulfillment?

Perhaps a guidance counselor can be of help in self-assessment. Another approach that has worked for many people is to do the self-assessment exercises in *What Color Is Your Parachute: A Practical Manual for Job Hunters & Career-Changers* (by Richard Nelson Bolles, Ten Speed Press, published annually). Conversations with friends and relatives can also help a great deal. Regardless of how you go about this step of self-assessment, you should do it carefully, repeatedly, and over an extended period of time.

Choosing a career path is one of the most important series of actions of you will ever perform. Where the outcome is of great importance, the economic way of thinking suggests you should make a large effort to get the best information you can and to critically evaluate this information. Some information is easy to get, the kind you find on computer databases and in reference books such as the *Occupational Outlook Handbook,* the *Dictionary of Occupational Titles*, and the *Guide for Occupational Exploration*. Aptitude and vocational-interest tests, conferences (several, over a period of months or years) with a guidance counselor, and reference books are good beginnings, but this information is limited in usefulness because it is dry and general and can only suggest answers to the essential question: "Would I be happy doing this kind of a job for many years?"

If you're thinking of being an accountant, for example, you would want to know whether you are good with figures, what the average annual salaries are for beginning accountants, what are the types of jobs they do, and what are the opportunities for career advancement. If you enjoy your accounting classes and get high grades in them, that would be a significant clue that accounting might be a good career for you. But what you really need to know before going too far with an accounting major is what it is like to be an accountant, what the satisfactions and frustrations of the job are, and whether this is a job that you would probably grow to like more as the years go by. Often, people either grow to like their jobs more and more as they gain experience over the years, or they gradually get to hate their jobs more and more as time goes by.

In earlier and simpler times, children often followed in their parents' footsteps. To some extent, this still happens today. For instance, the sons and daughters of doctors are much more likely to become doctors than are those whose parents do not practice medicine. If you have a parent, older sibling, or aunt or uncle or other relative who does a job that you think you might like, information from this person can be of great value. For one thing, these people are likely to know something about you and to care about you, and they are likely to be truthful. If one of your parents, older brothers or sisters, or other relatives finds a career particularly fulfilling, maybe you should take a close look at it.

While in college, many students become overwhelmed with classes, studies, and other responsibilities and activities. The merely urgent demands on your time may drive out some of the truly important activities in your life. You can always postpone talking to a guidance counselor, or setting up a summer internship, or studying books about career choice. My suggestion to deal with this problem is to budget some time during the first days of each term, and also during Christmas and summer vacations for thinking and taking action about fundamental issues such as career choice. In particular, the week before New Year's Day is a good time to re-evaluate who you are, where you have been going, and in what direction you would like to be going.

Economic logic dictates that you should recognize a *choice* for what it is, which is an action that has costs as well as benefits. For choices having to do with choosing a career and finding a job, you should not drift into the path of least resistance, nor should you become immobilized by the flood of information and uncertainty that surrounds us all.

To deal with career choices in an uncertain world, what we need to do is to gain knowledge and understanding of how economies work, to develop skills of critical thinking, and to become proficient in dealing with words, graphs, and numbers. These general skills are helpful in getting good and interesting jobs, and they are general enough to apply to almost any career path. Furthermore, a study of economics is one of the best ways to develop general thinking skills. You don't have to become an economist to benefit from the concepts and skills you will learn in economics.

Evaluating Advice

We live in an uncertain world where judging the quality of advice is essential to making good choices. One of the most important abilities you can develop to survive and thrive in this world of imperfect information and changing reality is learning how to evaluate information. Your mechanic tells you that your car needs $700 worth of repairs. Your doctor tells you that you need to take a prescription drug to deal with the sleeplessness caused by the stress of student life. Are your mechanic and your doctor giving honest and competent advice? You are not an expert on automobiles or on medicine or on career choice, so how can you evaluate the advice of a mechanic or a doctor or a guidance counselor?

One of the surest ways to mess up your life is to accept advice uncritically. There are more than a few dishonest mechanics and doctors out there. In my opinion, however, the greatest hazards to your vehicle, your health, and your happiness in choice of a career, come from the advice of well-meaning but incompetent advisors. Perhaps guidance counselors are just as competent, on average, as doctors and mechanics. So what? *Get a second opinion.* Get third opinions, and more than three, when there is much uncertainty and an important choice in your life. The evaluation of information is one of the highest-level and most important skills you can learn, not only for choosing a career but also for doing well in it.

To sum up, where there is much uncertainty and where the choice is important, economic logic says you should spend a considerable amount of time, effort, and probably some money to get good information and to get a lot of it. You should compare the information and advice you get from various sources. Information cannot eliminate uncertainty, because we always make choices on the basis of expectations about the future. Of course, the future has not happened yet, so nobody can have perfect knowledge of what the outcomes of choices will be. What the critical evaluation of good information can do is to reduce uncertainty to manageable proportions and thus help you to make good choices.

Chapter 8
Savings, Debt, Budgeting, and Being Able to Sleep at Night

Where Does Your Money Go?

Information is important, not only for making big choices, such as choosing a career, but also for control of your personal finances. Besides unsatisfactory relationships and health problems, there is probably no greater source of worry, stress, and unhappiness in American lives than money and debt problems. Many people have a tendency to spend and borrow too much to be able to sleep well at night. (Some people have the opposite tendency, to save too much and to spend too little to enjoy life. They are relatively few in number.)

How can you get control of your finances? First of all, you need to know where your money goes. This information is not hard to get. If you have a checking account, your check register should have a record of payments and deposits. For cash purchases, you can save all the receipts you get for a month and stuff them into a resealable sandwich bag, along with scraps of paper that tell the amount and purpose of cash expenditures for which you don't have a receipt. Try to put your receipts and other notes of cash spending into the bag each evening, because you can usually remember at the end of the day how much you pumped into vending machines and whether you sent out for pizza. Then, at the end of the month, with your checkbook, calculator, and bag of receipts at hand, it takes less than an hour to divide your expenses into seven to ten categories and add up what you are spending for education, food, transportation (including car insurance), housing, medical and dental expenses, utilities, entertainment, gifts and donations, and so on. After keeping track of expenses for a few months you will have a record of where your money goes, and then you can stop recording every dollar you spend, unless your spending pattern changes or you happen to enjoy budgeting.

You may argue that budgeting is a waste of time, because your problem is that your income is simply too low to meet your expenses. This point of view is questionable, because good information can almost always clarify the nature of a financial problem and perhaps suggests directions to go to deal with the problem. In the absence of records on spending, you may lapse into the bad habit of self-deception. In other words, you may fool yourself into thinking your problems result merely from bad luck (car trouble, unexpected health expenses, overpriced textbooks, expenses connected to a friend's wedding, etc.), rather than from more fundamental problems. Economic logic says that you need good information to make good choices. The *only* way to get information on your income and spending is through budgeting.

Borrowing and Saving as Allocating Consumption over Time

When you borrow money, you are making a choice to consume more in the present in return for consuming less in the future, when you repay the debt by reducing future consumption. When you save, you are choosing less consumption today in return for more in the future. Most of us would like to consume more right now, and hence there is a tendency to save too little and to borrow too much. Excessive borrowing is much like drug addiction in that the habit brings short-term pleasure and long-term grief. Does it follow that you should not borrow at all?

Probably not: Most of us can be better off with *some* borrowing. For durable goods (such as autos or household appliances) that last longer than it takes to pay the debt that financed their purchase, borrowing often makes sense. In financing durable goods, what you're doing is paying for them as you use them. The benefits of enjoying these goods sooner rather than later may be far greater than the costs of the interest charges you pay. For some purchases, such as a home, almost everybody has to borrow to finance the purchase.

There is a problem to beware of, however, in financing purchases of homes, cars, and other long-lasting goods. This problem is that the availability of credit may encourage us to spend more on these items than they are worth to us. If the new-car salesperson tells you about the easy sixty-month payment plan (with a limited-time offer of cash rebates and a special low interest rate to first-time buyers!), you may all too easily fall into the trap of borrowing as much as you can. The large number of consumer bankruptcies and the widespread unhappiness associated with excessive debt show that many consumers do not make good choices in regard to using credit.

Is Borrowing Money to Finance an Education a Good Choice?

I can answer this question with a firm, decisive, and emphatic, "Maybe." If the education you get raises your lifetime income substantially, then getting student loans (and perhaps borrowing as much as you can) can be a good choice. On the other hand, suppose you end up with a college degree and tens of thousands of dollars in student loans, and then find that for years after graduation the best job you can get pays only two dollars an hour over the minimum wage. In that case, you would have been better off (from a financial standpoint) not going to college at all.

The evidence is that a college degree does pay off in much higher lifetime earnings for those with degrees, compared to those who lack degrees. Thus, for most students, it does make sense to borrow to finance education.

What about all those student loans? Wouldn't it make more sense to work your way through college and avoid all that debt? Probably not. Before you have a degree, your wages will most likely be rather low. On the other hand, your expected wages after graduation are likely to be much higher than they were before you get a degree. Thus, there is a good chance that you'll have to work far fewer hours to finance your education by repaying debt than you would by working before and during college. Especially questionable is the practice of taking a semester or a year off from school "to save up for tuition and college expenses." You may save a few thousand dollars, but by postponing graduation you have lost the opportunity to earn much higher wages at an earlier point in your life.

Being Able to Sleep at Night

The great advantage of budgeting is that by increasing your information you can reduce uncertainty and worry about money matters. For peace of mind, you need to follow three financial guidelines. First, you should not spend more than your finances (earnings, gifts, and prudent borrowing) permit. Second, you should have a cash reserve for expenses that seem to pop up out of nowhere, like expenses for health care, repair or replacement of appliances, speeding tickets, and other drains on your funds that may or may not occur. Finally, you should have a good credit rating. These three elements go together.

By budgeting you can know what your position is and whether you need to take steps to either decrease spending or increase your sources of funds. Because of uncertainty, you do need a cash reserve. One of the main reasons to save money is to have an emergency fund to deal with occasional expenses, that can hit you one, two, three, during the space of a few weeks and put you down in a pit of unpaid bills. This cash reserve need not be large. There is a world of difference between having a few hundred dollars in savings and having none. Now, what about a good credit rating?

A credit rating is based on a history of repaying debt. Thus, your credit rating reflects your financial reputation. The key to a good credit rating is to avoid excessive debt and to pay bills on time. To get a credit rating at all, you do need to borrow, at least occasionally, and then demonstrate that you can and will repay your debts. Having a substantial amount of unused credit can add to peace of mind and to your ability to sleep at night, just as having some money in a savings account can. A good rule for credit cards is to pay the balance in full at the end of each month, so as to avoid interest charges and also to show ability and willingness to repay debt. If you will not be able to repay in full at the end of the month, perhaps you should not use a credit card for a purchase, or perhaps you should not make the purchase at all.

Chapter 9
Personal Investing

Tradeoffs Everywhere

Suppose you have money to invest, perhaps in a pension fund over which you have some control. How can you get maximum safety and maximum return on your investment? You can't. The surest finding of financial economics is that there is a tradeoff between risk and return. A very risky investment (for instance, in a new real estate development) may have a high expected rate of return, but there is also a good chance that it will turn into a turkey. Relatively safe investments, such as bank accounts, government savings bonds, and certificates of deposit *always* have a relatively low rate of return. Indeed, after subtracting for income taxes and inflation, the rate of return on "safe" investments may be zero or below zero.

Now you may not want to believe this dismal fact. You may think you can make a lot of money by being smarter than other investors. Perhaps you think that by taking lots of classes in finance or by listening and watching for new information, you must be able to get rich with little risk. Sorry, no way. The basic message of the infomercials on TV that tell you how to get rich quick is a lie. Furthermore, one of the fastest ways to lose your money is to act on the basis of inside information, because plenty of other people have it too.

The question, "If you're so smart, why aren't you rich?" has been asked of more than one economist. (The snappiest reply was by Nobel Prize winning economist Paul Samuelson, who came back with, "If you're so rich, why aren't you smart?") The short answer to the question is that being smart has little to do with becoming rich. You can find a readable discussion of this topic in an interesting one-page article by economist Donald McCloskey, titled "An Economic Uncertainty Principle" (*Scientific American*, November 1994, p. 107).

Do all these discouraging facts mean that economics is worthless when it comes to investing money? Not at all. What economics can help people do is to recognize limits and to get a good rate of return, within the limits of what is possible. In other words, studying economics won't help you to get rich quick, but it can help you plan for financial security, keep you from losing your shirt, and prevent you from losing sleep over your investments.

Getting Rich Slowly

There are two sure things in financial markets. First, they will fluctuate, sometimes wildly. Second, many people want to believe that they can get rich quick. Because of this wishful thinking, an unending flood of bad advice rushes by us in the form of new books, newsletters, magazines, infomercials, computer information services, and so on, all of which are telling you that *yes*, you can make a ton of money in a hurry. The people making the money are the ones selling this advice and the ones collecting commissions from the gullible sheep who follow various get-rich-quick paths to the shearing pens. These get- rich-quick schemes are all one kind or another of speculation.

Speculation is a gamble, a project or a purchase or a strategy that may pay off big, *if everything goes right*. Once in a while, everything does, and so every now and then a successful speculator hits the jackpot. This success requires the same kind of luck that winning the Publishers Clearinghouse Sweepstakes does. Unless you want to gamble, avoid speculation. If you do like to gamble, the odds offered at Las Vegas or Atlantic City casinos are as good as (and often better than) those offered by real estate, commodity, and stock speculations.

Betting on short-term movements in the stock market is a form of gambling, and so is betting on bond prices to go up or down. Nobody can forecast these fluctuations with any degree of reliability for at least two reasons. First, financial markets move on the basis of expectations. These expectations, based on hope and fear, greed and panic, can turn on a dime, and nobody can predict which way they will go. How and why expectations behave as they do is more the subject of social psychology than of economics. Neither sociologists nor psychologists, however, have any answers that would help to predict movements in stock and bond prices. A second reason for the unpredictability of short-term movements in financial markets is that these fluctuations resemble what economists call a "random walk." In other words, the day-to-day or month-by-month fluctuations of interest rates or of stock prices are random and unpredictable. Both evidence and economic theory support the random walk hypothesis.

On the other hand, given data from the past hundred years, we can say that a widely based average of common stocks tends to go up considerably faster than the rate of inflation *over a period of many years*. In other words, if you can invest in a diversified assortment of stocks, and if the next forty years resembles the past century in regard to return on investments, then you may do well with one of the simplest of all possible investment strategies. This strategy takes into account two essential findings of economics concerning limitations to knowledge. First, we cannot predict short-term price fluctuations, and second, we cannot pick individual stocks that will outperform the market. Here's the strategy, in two parts.

First, use dollar cost averaging to minimize risk from stock market fluctuations. The idea behind dollar cost averaging is to put the same amount of money per month (or per paycheck, or per calendar quarter) into buying stocks. When stock prices are low, you automatically buy more, and when they are high, you automatically buy fewer shares than you did at lower prices. How is this possible? Well, suppose you invest one hundred dollars per month. The number of dollars you put in stays the same, but the number of shares you buy each month changes, as shown in the following example.

Month	Price per share	Amount invested	Number of shares purchased
January	$1.00	$100	100
February	$ 2.00	$100	50
March	$ .50	$100	200

Total amount invested is $300, but you purchased 350 shares, because you purchased far more at the lower price of $.50 per share than at the higher prices. The beauty of dollar cost averaging is that you can make stock market fluctuations work for you instead of against you. (One note of caution: Dollar cost averaging to buy an assortment of stocks will produce good results only in cases where the long-term trend of stock prices is flat or rising. Just because stock prices have risen over every twenty year period for which we have records, there is no guarantee that the long-term trend will continue to be up.)

Now, what about diversification? How can an investor who can save only $100 per month buy a broad assortment of stocks? A common stock index fund offers an easy, low-cost way to achieve a broad diversity of purchases of common stocks. These index funds invest in a very wide assortment of the stocks of hundreds or thousands of companies. Hence, the performance of the fund will be the same as that of a broadly based index of stocks, 500, or 3,000, or even 5,000 different common stocks. Investing in an index fund recognizes the limitation to our knowledge set by the impossibility of picking a stock or a group of stocks that will outperform market averages.

The fees involved in purchasing and managing index funds can be quite low (much lower than for most kinds of investments). Thus, your money can be working for you rather than being eaten up by commissions and various kinds of charges. Many advisors encourage people to put money into plans that carry high commissions or management fees or other kinds of charges. Economic logic says you should ask yourself whether such advice reflects attention to *your* best interest or to the interest of the advisor. If a broker or financial planner or other source of investment advice seems unenthusiastic about my simple advice, saying, "Why get rich slowly when you can buy my product and get rich quick?", you should ask yourself whether this lack of enthusiasm for buying an index fund with dollar cost averaging may be connected to the level of fees involved with different kinds of investments.

You won't get rich quick by buying shares in a common stock index fund with dollar cost averaging, but neither will you be likely to kiss your savings good-bye. You can follow the strategy I recommend with no newsletters, little investment of time, and no worry, once you learn to ignore market fluctuations.

Note that the alternative to getting rich slowly is not getting rich quickly. The alternative to getting rich slowly is not to get rich at all. In a growing economy, such as U.S. economy, everyone who can earn a decent income and save ten or twelve percent of it each year over thirty years or so can look forward to a comfortable retirement, provided they do not lose their assets from inflation or speculation. The alternative to getting rich slowly is a bleak future of scrimping and scraping by on Social Security benefits for the last decades of your life, which is not something pleasant to contemplate.

Chapter 10
Human Capital as Your Most
Important Asset

In societies based on farming, land is the key source of wealth. In economies based on industry, the ownership of buildings and equipment is the main distinction between the haves and the have-nots. Today we live in an information economy, where the ability to learn and apply specialized knowledge is more and more becoming the main distinction between those who enjoy high incomes and those who do not.

Capital produces a stream of income because it is a productive asset. If you have more capital, then you can expect to have more income. Land and machinery are still valuable assets, but nowadays they require much specialized knowledge to make them highly productive. Making financial investments and saving some of your income, as discussed in the previous chapter, can help you to get rich slowly so as to enjoy retirement with a decent income. But there is one way to increase your income more rapidly than saving ten or twelve percent of it for thirty or more years. The name of this prescription for increasing your income is *investing in human capital,* and you are doing it right now, by reading this booklet and by taking a course in economics. There are several kinds of investment in human capital that can have a large impact on your future income.

Health and Migration

Spending money and changing habits to improve your health are two of the most productive investments in human capital you can make.

Healthy and energetic people can be far more productive than sickly and tired ones. Perhaps this point is obvious, but many people ignore obvious facts despite their importance. One of the reasons that people in poor countries have such low incomes is that they are sick much of the time. Even in prosperous countries, many people do not deal with their medical problems, sometimes for financial reasons, sometimes for other reasons. If your health is excellent, do your best to keep it that way. If you have some condition that should receive medical intervention, then get help.

Suppose you live in a rural area or some other part of the country where economic opportunities lag behind those available in the prosperous metropolitan areas. In such cases, to achieve a higher income the best investment you can make may be a one-way bus ticket to an area of greater prosperity. If you choose to stay in a place with few good job opportunities, you have made a choice to accept a relatively low income. Now, there is nothing wrong or irrational with choosing a low income or even voluntary poverty in return for other considerations. If you want to get away from the rat race of traffic congestion, air pollution, high crime rates, and high housing costs, you can do this by going to a rural county that is losing population. Again, it is a matter of tradeoffs. If you seek higher income and more chances for career advancement, then you must be willing to go where the better opportunities are. And where are they? With relatively few exceptions, the jobs that pay the most are in or close to major metropolitan areas, and particularly in areas that are growing faster than the national average.

Education as the Biggest Investment in Human Capital

College graduates earn far more over their lifetimes than do those without college degrees. There are at least two reasons behind this finding. First, many students actually do learn some useful thinking skills, knowledge, and habits of self-discipline from their years in college. Second, college acts as a screening and sorting device to separate highly motivated and more intellectually able people (who tend to get degrees) from less motivated and less intelligent people (who tend not to attend college or to drop out). Employers reserve almost all their good jobs for those with college degrees, and regardless of how bright, how experienced, and how energetic you are, your chances of getting an interview for a good job are slim to none unless you have or are about to get a college degree.

Please do not misunderstand me. I am *not* claiming that a degree provides a guarantee of a good job. On the contrary, what the evidence shows is that lack of a degree disqualifies you from consideration for almost all good jobs. You may earn a Ph.D. in economics and find that the best job you can get is as a letter carrier. There is no guarantee that investment in education will pay off for a particular individual in terms of high earnings, job security, or career advancement. On the average, however, investment in higher education has paid off quite well during the past half century. Indeed, there is strong evidence that the pay gap between those with and those without college degrees increased rapidly during the 1980s.

The first wisdom of economics is that choices have costs. The choice to attend college comes with the cost of lost earnings during the years when a student is putting time into attending class and studying rather than working. Is it worthwhile to lose earnings now in return for a probability of much higher earnings in the future? That is a question only you can answer for yourself, though economic data can suggest what the terms of the tradeoff are for large numbers of people during past decades.

Choices have not only costs but also benefits, and the noneconomic benefits of attending college may be at least as large as the higher expected lifetime earnings. Understandably, economists don't pay as much attention to "non-economic" factors such as gaining new friends, learning lifetime sports, or becoming intellectually alive as they do to the benefits and costs that can be expressed in dollar terms. Nevertheless, these possible nonmonetary benefits of your years of college may be as important as the benefits that money measures. Good choices reflect an evaluation of all relevant benefits and costs, not just the ones that economists can measure.

Chapter 11
Conclusion

What does economics have to offer you? I think it can offer you a great deal, if you are willing to put in the time and effort it takes learn this way of thinking. Two great benefits stand out. First, economics can help you to make sense out of the world, of what has happened, is happening, and is likely to happen. The ability to understand the economic world and to see patterns in events can be a great advantage for you. Many people see the world as a confusing, chaotic place, where everything is a jumble of personalities, disasters, and meaningless numbers. Economic concepts can help you to understand and to evaluate economic news and thereby protect yourself against and also take advantage of long-term trends.

Second, studying economics can help you learn to think better, both in terms of words and in terms of numbers. The habit of critical thinking is a pearl beyond price, and no discipline is better than economics at developing practice in skills and habits of critical thinking. Another great advantage of economics classes (especially those beyond the introductory level) is that they can help you to learn to think quantitatively in terms of numbers, percentages, graphs, and mathematics. People who can think in terms of both words and numbers have a great advantage over those who cannot, when it comes to making good choices. To understand the world and to help you make good choices, that's where a study of economics can help you.